The

Watch

The poetry and art of
Jonathan Ojanpera

The Watch

Copyright Jonathan Ojanpera May, 2014

ISBN # 978-0-692-21614-9

Published by Jonathan Ojanpera

www.johnnyojanpera.wordpress.com

Cover photo © Natali S. Bravo 2014

This book is dedicated to my wife, Lisa and to my four daughters. Without their support none of this would have been possible.

The Poet's Heart

As if I knew the source, your point of
fury
Nightfall ushers in your haunted
inking
If I could call out the heat, suffer it's
will
I may know solace, know I'm not
sinking

The dark belongs to your nocturnal
spell
Your treatise of pain, my fear's
manifesto
Imbibed in love or ecstasy, I write it
back

I imply and mimic 'til I've no place to
go

Forever in wonder at how I shake as
mad
Every line a shock to my shaded
center
Your harmony holds me, know it by
rote
I, without a light will never see to
enter

So tell me once, a hint, just one
spoiler
As to how you pour out my soul as
well
Effortless flash of brilliance, true

intuit

I can only make sense of what you tell

Elemental

We materialize only to be vaporized
All rise up, to better see the bottom
Our soft landing pending, hanging

Fire under foot, shoelaces in soot
Penning the carnage to escape it
Looking for a clue just to stop it

Raining ice, toxic, from pure waters
Painting the pictures to preserve it
Won't be hanging on wealthy walls

We vaporize only to be materialized
Staring up at something much better
Graceful flight pending, anticipating

Drowning Patience

Bottom of the sea, looking up
I see all you people swim
While I struggle to breathe
Down with the urchins
Coral, anemones
All of you act, live free
As if life is free of enemies
My enemy capsized me
No life boat, no rescue team
Fear creeps in, crippling scene
I understand the depths, unseen
To you, to them, helpless indeed
Still I wait, this impossible dream
If the one who loves me
Would ever take the leap
She dropped a shell, hit me square
Should call it hope, more likely
For I am far too deep
She won't see me
Even when masked, if at all
Into the blue, sight is blurred

I have grown weary
No voices will be heard
Waited long enough
Last laboured breath
Comes to me, rope
Fleet of hope felt
Death resigned
Dream of the surface
Realize as I rise
How long I waited
Pulled from my salty lair
Air, the prize, ocean bare

Escape

If I could escape this memory
These pictures in satin white
I may find my way into night

Energize me or execute me
This balance is rigged too
Why not give, release true

Tired of running in plain sight
A new moon black, then back
I beg you, untie me from the rack

When I go I warn, don't follow
This time, I must leave your crypt
No longer reading, living the script

Freedom depends upon my speed

Knowing fear as this spells death

I ask again, leave me, my breath

If you were certain, really true

Merely human, see like I do

This haunt in my mind is you

For Peace

For peace I would give all I have
gained
To escape the crushed and melted
elements
Hide in their native domains, man
deplete
These roads, these curbs mean
nothing but noise
Great structures all stolen from
mother, no poise

For peace I would quiet every
machine hum
Never looking back to the motors run
drum
I would go to my place where iron is

formed

Where veins of gold remain unscathed

Never a road carved from mountain's
stone

For peace I would silence the sirens
and bells

Neon, fluorescent, shatter the colored
spells

I know of this place lit only by flame

Austere by nature, consumed in her
warmth

The night will keep me, silent
embrace

For peace I would take you away
from the clatter

Chatter, inane rattle, mind shaking

babble

We can walk there or run, time has

come

Should have been years since we left

the 'civil'

Exacting my dream will surely bring

order

Penned

Penned words, "only words", she said
I believed her as I do every one
spoken
For she can speak no wrong, not to
me
Her voice makes pictures, I know sure

I wonder now, if I only pen them for
not
Do they belong to the wind, for no ear
A race to report a past long behind us
Inking dead trees for an unknown eye

Perhaps her reading is wrong, untrue
What if I drew a flying dove to behold

A blue-sky perfection and it's sun lit

These pictures could spell a future

As if my will alone gave life to love

Would will change her weary mind

Free to fly when the last stanza dries

Wings written, frozen in this, our time

Read me, my love, you may find my
words

They may just spell out what is to
come

Not of prophetic tongue, nor
prescience

But of a concentric peace, one inside
one

All New

Under this cruel sun, I found it

May have known emptiness

I suppose you've felt alone

Even the trembling of fear

Your bones may be convulsive

Perhaps the sleep of your heart

Nothing new here, I know this

You have been gifted helpless

As the sun blinds, I saw it too

The death of entwined souls

A moment true, still so real

The crux though, it is all new

To me or not to you, never mind

The sting has never felt this way

A searing of the lungs, poisoned

Blood turned blue, it's all so new

When they say to me, no truth

I can say back, I've the proof

The sun, the moon know too

All of this pain is perfectly new

In Case I Forget

When I lost her, I forgot
The girl stopped, looked
Knew how many lives had passed

Must have been thousands
She knew my way
Taught her dismay

She never turns away
Though I leave, unreceived
No matter, hearts bled

In my passion boils hate
No more running 'bout
Innocence lost, clean slate

Received her with doubt
Funny thing, my sway
Attraction magnetic

Of all the girls passing my way
There is but one, loves to play
Life she saved, five times in days

So if you wonder why I stay
Tell yourself it goes both ways
Angel and devil into the fray

In case I forget the *one* by me
I'll remember none the misery
Though vows tattered, it will be

Ink

the ink made me spill
flowers, and maybe a vase
no reason at all

there is no reason
swimming in madness fits me
as if reason was

ink black is preferred
invisible me, hidden
nothing here is free

the colors you see
they break the spell easily
still, you won't find me

Life, Blood

Angel true, keeper of this life

Though a thread keeps me hanging

Allows me to channel the strife

I tried to slice it, cut it through

She clutched her end, pulled me to

Holds me tight, lover's grasp

Still I fight her, cut the string

The life I detest, I fear no more

Left in the goodness

Of another's strangled soul

She made the call, but to save

Never asked, never a call

She saw the thread, such gall

Born to be transparent to all

To all but her vision, I can tell

Intuit missed, her siren call

This one was different

No boat, no rocks, no songs

A simple thread holds me

While the angel acts, nothing at all

Effortless my weight, let me fall

Miracles

If ever a miracle were found
It would be miraculous too

If only death weren't a race
It could be won evermore

Oh my soul, sinner pure
Death can't catch me

Too many souls
Crying out, so

Miracles do
Never will

Save me
Nor you

Again

Amen

Purchase

Would anyone like to purchase a boy?

His weight has grown heavy inside

I've really no use for the offer he

made

Playing, pretending that all is of fun

There is no time to tend to his laugh

Never a moment for a timid glance

I've found no purpose in keeping

He only pulls me back to the past

If he exists as my artist, or a muse

Surely I will profit from his selling

A great exchange, he is only a pest

Surely one wants what's in there

He requires no sitter, no real care

I have starved him for many years

Yet he remains, pestering my soul

Won't someone please take this boy

Obsidian

She turned to me, her eyes, hazel
Refracting blues and grays
So bright, past lucent

I tried to look past the reflections
The myriad of gems
Sun's light, too bright

As the day turned to dusk
Her eyes followed suit
Color diminished, dark

Lost in obsidian, black-smoke glass
I realize now, the truth within
No way in, not even in sin

My choices are two, black or white

The black I cannot penetrate

The white no more than light

Illumination comes in time

Not even this can attempt to pry

Her broken soul, lost as I

Surrender

He asked me to step back, relent and
yield
The only reply I could find was
opposition

The matter was one of debate, not of
fates
A lesser man, I could find no way to
move

He spoke of having the advantage
over me
The funny thing is, he was right, but
wrong

The odds are designed to be played,
chance

If I surrendered now, how could I
ever know

To win or compete plays no role, not
a one

The advantage lies within our natural
law

You see, he had offered me no proof
or fact

If this be my final act, so may it be in
truth

His dripping-wisdom residue left a
mark

Made me remember that truth wasn't
his

This surrender an impossibility for
certain
Please, sir I ask, relent, step back and
yield

The Gypsy Life

There is a man
His name is Truth
He has but one companion
Her name is Honesty
A nomadic duet from
Ancient times
Homeless and starving
Throughout their lives
Beaten and tattered
They uncover yet
Another passing refuge
The time is well spent
Their wounds covered over
Like a fresh spring morning
With bees that hover
Above brilliant honeysuckles
And the fields they cover
This glorious reign is
Most often short-lived
Now it's time to be on their way
Mirth will come

One distant and blessed day
Two beautiful beings
Immortal, unheard
Yet so easily destroyed
In the utterance of a single word.

Unbuttoned

The day passed, missing your
affection
Touch eluded, taste, great allusion
If I hadn't seen you, it may be another
You languish in lonely, now passive
Only missing your fate, ghost white
lover
Twin desire, meeting with strangeness
As if new, perhaps my first,
willingness
Purity was never becoming of me
anyway
You tell me I am no more than a slut
That our meeting is one of so many
Does it really matter tonight, here?
Call it a tryst, name me your call boy

Worth every pant, every sliding

finger-tip

This trip, laced with longing, every

drop

You're already unbuttoned, come in

Catch my stare as my head goes light

Eyes betray my desire, let me in, to

you

We've only hours 'til the light finds

us

This pink-tease indecision must hide

Let us be sated before alarms rise

To deny this skin numbing night play

Will only leave us heavy another day

One of water saved, no salty sweet

mess

Keep my promise of this, deep within

If not, I'll remind you, deep lover's

kiss

The Danger

We knew this was dangerous

The day we saw the deep
The way we kept our hearts
The same as we gave them

The white flag of our youth
Given in to the face of eternity
It never came easy, this thing

We knew this was dangerous

You knew we were only kids
I was too young to fear it
Never mind, we promised

We knew this was dangerous

Half a lifetime passed, we knew

Time had graced us with life

Forces pooled around our hearts

We knew this was dangerous

Silver Lining

With a micro-plate-tarnish silver
lining
The gift of life remains with a dark
twist
What if the charcoal swallows the
bliss

This lining does not float in the clouds
Will never even hover near the
ground
It is in you, in you fighting to stay in

If the dust it settles, I'll know the way
The way to extract the black, the mold
The shit caught inside you will be
mine

I speak from a low place, confused,
cold
If I had any power at all, I may be
bold
But the silver has no lustre, value now

I will mine to the bottom, the very
depths
One scoop at a time, find the silver
vein
Take your black lungs as my only scar

What I need is one with yours you see
To run, to play, to take what we
please
This hard rocky coal must yield to us

Turned Out Me

I hear your plight
I feel sorry
I've got my own now
Can't really blame me

You could've said love
You should have said peace
You should have seen her
She even tried lace

No wonder she left you
Everyone knew
Now you're drowning
Swimming in blue

Had a nightmare

Four a.m.

Could never happen

But it turned out me

She must have told me

I was so close

I couldn't hear you

Gone, my rose

I should have seen it

Forever nose to nose

I must have missed it

Spelled simply in prose

The Artist's Flaw

Darkness falls, painter left unaware
The sinking into this realm
Leaves behind the prospect of peace
Her only choice is to follow a fine
trail
Though dark, she navigates delicate
turns
Brush strokes, finesse, never fails

Sinking into an empty page
The writer stares blank, knowing
Unknown devastated, must release
New moon black night, perfect state
Empty, alone, no soul can tap in
Life ahead depends on spilled ink

The musician holds his instrument

Begs for Inspiration that may not

come

His mind goes blank, enters the

downcast

The strings, infinite combinations his

cue

Esteem wilted by what came before

him

Finally he embraces shadows and

their tones

The artist sings the song of creation

The blackest, the empty, solitude

found

Mining his center, separates dusk

from dawn

Impossibility is her muse, maybe lost
infatuation

A crowd surrounds, see-through as
glass
Perhaps the artist's flaw will never
pass

The Script

Who filled these pages with death
Was it the power drunk, mind-blind
With no spirit watching over them
They seized our nature, caged us

How did they learn to write this way
Was it good or evil, benevolent
weevils
The masses let them scribble our fate
Locked in servitude, happy, satiate

I sought the missing page to read
aloud
Shocked, split and twisted at the
sound

Our fathers lied, propagated a utopia
A new civilization that wouldn't care

As the page read, eyes open, gaping
wide
A world they created with mother's
blood
I knew then that it couldn't last, but
then
A few escaped, exit stage right, corral

These few run free despite their rage
Awakening to wreckage every day
Sweet little freedom from the book
One page to start from, a new script

Structure

She is made of raw elements
Rare as virgin timber
Precious as iron ore

She is the shelter you seek
A lioness with teeth
Daughter of a storm

She is the passion you keep
Every secret is her's alone
Watches your breath in sleep

She listened when you spoke
Never told you how...still
Knows every note you wrote

She knew when you missed it

Her spirit closed, with a pardon

Your gaze, her only respite

She will only crave so long

As a structure in disrepair

Love her, strum her song

Mistaken

The last thing I saw was your root
beer eyes
The last thing I wanted was to see you
blink
Vibrance led to this purple-grey death
grip
I was soon mistaken as I cast my
intention
Beauty glistened, your blink yielded
to sleep
Time ceased in my world, motion, not
one
My sight, my navigator in perpetual
night
In the pause I plead, open them just
once
My essence fading fast, I crave your
light
We are meant to stand upright, not
prone
Me alone, laid to waste, our time

stolen
If I stand much longer, I will surely
drop
Don't leave me mistaken, hear my
voice
As you woke, my breath returned to
you
Hammered nail patient, no more for
me
As if your life was taken for cruel
intent
When you opened up, all faith was
dead
Thank the heavens or the gods for life
In this season, you weren't mistaken
Spring awaits you as I have been true
None but my love has ever saved you

Lines And What You Find In Between

Spilling your wanderings keeps me
guessing
A language I will never comprehend
My affection, my agony, the word
My commission to expel, pressing

Spitting your life at me leaves me
blind
Closed-book letters, locked in a void
Key-dance, tap along to write myself
Tell the story to me, refrain arcane,
mined

Speaking these things will net you not
Verses, antics no one gets, in vain

My guilt lies in obsession, never ease

My muse, my noose, white-fevered

hot

Your acidic love gone wrong is sweet

The solution you scribe is never

actual

Bear-trap buried, my ink streaks

pages

Scrub every word to catch a steady

beat

A matter of great import, say what

you will

The story can be told in meter, no

deception

What I bear is mine, poetic, possibly

so

The greats tell me to fancy the word,

be still

Lost The Way

We were lost in a twisting maze
Spheres, auras as beacons alight
Running away in half-moon haze
While our longing was meant to be

Memory correct serves you sure
That I sought in earnest that night
Our thoughts fancied a love so pure
While our longing was meant to be

As if destined, two found again
Ever searching with little light
As if the likes have always been
While our longing was meant to be

The Declaration

To fall into memory, the beginning of
time
Not soon after I declared war upon
you
It was merely poetic, and so we
thought

Soon my declaration, passion intoned
Impossible energy to master, so fast
Created war on earth, with another
sense

You heard me clearly, love and
indifference
They are lovers you see, never
enemies

Ours, a battle with me black, you
white

The war ended cold, casualties count
With only two left standing, who won
You would never tell, deny this well

Now I beg a truce, the fires
smoldering
A peace accord, a summit meeting
Whatever the cost to hear that voice

If I am your enemy, lull me in closer
Willing to be burned, blackened
Erase the folly of my declaration

Writing Damage

Throwing bones, it didn't stick
Consulting the witch only burned
The mystics failed in misery
Clergy fucked me, perfect fantasy

This damage is what remains
Evolution unchanged, only lack wings
Dance of the believer, adaption, claim
Cold war stalemate, devils sing

They dance 'round me, taunting
My being, my essence, already sold
Belief is their aim, can't be blamed
Unknowing, empty, blank in my
periphery

If I would speak to these deceptions

What more could I gain?

Empty, damaged, steeples blame

Tell me so, complete my denial

My teaching blooms from the vicars

All made it clear, facts askew

An apple, a boat, the possession

Fables in faith, eternity consumed

Writing this down confirms the birth

Not of greatness, but of fire, doom

A crowd numbing system of

assurance

Your book's not sufficient, black rose

bloom

Parallel

Heart and mind ever intersect

Infinite lines, parallel, must not exist

We lost ourselves, along with each
other

Disappeared for months, miles persist

As soon as you landed, I surfaced,
soaked

You must have been gliding,
windblown

The ocean's floor, my wilderness
abode

We shared a look, strangers in a bout
of love

Souls linked sure, clipped ribbons
here and there
You said it would pass without
reserve, repaired
When you spoke, your heart was in it,
believing
My mind moved in close, heart vying
to be even

Some part went missing, unaligned
hem
Ran to nowhere, crossed my mind on
the way
A heart jumping borders, a mind with
her
I need it back, before the weight is too
great

To chase it seems monumental, out of
sight
Seeing me now, her only piece of
what she lacks
Parallel, patient, we brush by and wait
Run these lines for awhile, the rest
will be back

Must Be Honey

For seconds or hours, we adhere
Not to laws of science nor gods
Only to our impulse, as captive

Not a motion, not of that world
Heat standing, no want for more
The touch is where we find it all

As if skin were bejeweled, marked
With none apparent, sticky drops
Must be honey, most sugary pure

Drawn in weightless calm beauty
If I pull away, you remain with me
If I stay, succulent becomes sultry

Inevitable slide as snow it melts

Translucent glue yields to charm

Temptation blooms fascination

Must be honey finding my tongue

Greatest frailty is keeping us near

Seconds to hours most sugary pure

Pressed Flowers

A life full of color is what we seek
The drab and colorless, often weep
We all draw color from other life
Wilting into death all the same

Flowers draw color from death
The exhumed remains of the like
We outlast their blooms at a price
What price is worth this ashenness

If we were further pressed as they
Immortality may come to us as well
A permanent fixture on your wall
Never any need to bother you at all

I could simply look pretty as a peony
Wouldn't speak out like most, at will
No need to feed me with loving words
Who could hear behind glass likewise

So press me tight, between two boards
Be sure to frame me in your best
colors
I'll live for, eternity 'til the glass
cracks
Holding the tones that I certainly lack

Raven's Lore

I light wherever I may, you stare as if
my prey
The beast to take you, a creature to
glare
As the story goes, I am to greet you
Judge you, steal you, hide you, damn
you
I tell you, the lines seldom bare me
true
For I am a simple fowl, black as my
down
Myth and fairy tale paint me in a
darker coat
Your stories lie in envy, and in
cretinous fear
For to fly from your advance, must be
exacting
Elusive you make me, scarce you will
see me
When you find me on the perimeter
fence

Fear may grip you, my refinement
catch you
My true acts of genius come in two
ways
Bewitching from a tree's top, staring
out
Fluttering in blackest night, sight
without
If these be named magic, devilry or
illusion
Let the sorcerers do also their works
Leave it to the wizards, the gin, the
witches
I am merely a black feathered drifter
With intent innocent, designed by
Mother
She gave me cover, keen sense of
danger
Never intended, your fear is my
nature

Sound

Song is a sense of life

Sound, the rites of balance

Singing brings us closer

Synonymous with grace

Sending us to new worlds

Sliding into a dance

Standing in passion's land

Consequence

The moment I caught a look at her
almond eyes
Of burnished bronze, cinnamon,
ginger artistry
There stared the telling of my infinite
weakness

If ever a dare were made, it was she,
doubled
Never a word spoken, and no real
need for one
We met eyes and spoke every
meaning in spirit

My countenance, my world, defined
emergent

So new as to drape a tapestry of fear
over me
A dismay at the occurrence of sharing
her soul

An introduction of chance worth
every lifetime
A summit meeting, one reaping
consequence
None the wiser, we ignored,
dismissed a love

What happening surrounding this act
of vice
Became our left-lean, drunken stupor
bliss
This melting smolder pot of
permanence

The days went by without any thought
of time

The result of a silly accord, the
accident royale

A consequence unseen, intrinsic
bound deed

Feels Like

For words like ecstasy, heaven
Understating, underwhelming
Numbing, shaking, perfection
They are only words to reflect
As if through a dirty window
For the sake of passion, null
Heavy breath, slightest touch
Beads of sweat break through
It's you, it's me who know how
To keep these words in books
I could never tell what happens
Would never explain the fires
Night and day they burn high
Time cannot dull, nor quench
Our own church, worship two
Spirits collide, our souls slide
Into the dimension we made
We merely show up and dance
You see me as the only one
I look ever more to you
Behind closed door

Under cover light
Ending world
We'll sing
Waltz
You
Me

Heat Sense

Pre-dawn, shivering window breeze
Stolen blankets and my frozen skin
Dare to move closer out of my need

She was the thief, the sole perpetrator
Guilty association, caution dispelled
Under cover thaw, my only move now

That's when I saw you, and the first
Reprieve from an ice weakened sun
I vow not to shiver, a shock on skin

Bury my face deep into your neck
Wrapping every limb, even closer
Your perpetual heat takes me over

Her response is decided, pushing

As if I were seen first, then invited

Half-sleep slow dance transform

Intertwined, as we become one

This keen sense of heat realized

We sleep again, maybe 'til noon

Dans les points de suture

{In stitches}

We could speak of cuts inflicted
I could tell you so many times
Whether it be by sword or dagger
You divided my body, hewn pure

We could battle for land taken
I could swallow yours whole
As if belonging to the gentry
My lands gifted, grudge demure

We could talk about who's been
bleeding
My body is near empty, pooled,

immersed

As if you took no damage, only

offense

The puddles, a compound, toxic

assured

We could fight it all out, right the

wrong

Needle pricks, nail holes, damage

replete

Scarring communal, look at us now

Disarm your battalion, memory is

blurred

We can unpack the dressings, cutting

cease

Cleanse the wounds, sew the openings

Cover the stitching with a touch,

maybe more

If then you are ready, an incantation, a

cure

Claim The Storm

I always thought that Mother decided

When her children need water

Or sun rays, undivided

This storm came through

Just as I woke

Couldn't help but wonder

Why the clouds broke

Was it her morning duty

Imparting gray beauty

Or a sign of release

A symbol of tears not cried

Maybe this weight unleashed

If there were a storm I could claim

This is the one, I yield to blame

Be it her love setting me free

The way her touch speaks to me

Mother knows why

Permission given

I am the flood, raging sky

I won't give it back

'Til I am certain of this

Take shelter for awhile

The torrent's gush…

Fits And Starts

Strained speech, erratic action
I crave your presence, but then
You could be my enemy, and
Battles ensue, love or peace

The choice is not mine, add
A pace, one you cannot keep
So I run alone, won't stop
Then I stop, start to wait

My mind is made up, but
Then again, I can't decide
By my side, then step aside
Guess my move, left or flight

Pressure building, you tell me
Cry it out with perpetual dry
Eyes, grit, cathartic, but why
Sobs come hushed, hidden

Tell me, speak this clearly to
The sky, wonder why, not me
I can't process love or light
Paw at the darkness, sight

Valley floor and highest peak
I prefer one today, another, and
It doesn't make sense because
I only function in fits and starts

Her Black Rose

A thousand flowers to trample, a thousand songs to sing. Lovely destruction is all I have to give. I will never be her saint, for my presence may only bring a start, even a frightening bomb-blast-evolution to fearlessness. My scent is that of a rose strewn meadow, yet I am the color of old death. My strength lies in my own darkness; darkness that cradles her in peace. I am the sin that she carries. I am the freedom path she walks. I am the soft landing in her depths.

A death angel in a sense, though she can rest in her light, hear the telling notes of symphonies spilling from my lips like fresh rain. She knows my beauty despite my crimes. She sees through my hate to find shelter in love. Never a question asked of my methods, only acceptance; the proof lies in my history, in my immortality.

I am her black rose
yet so completely alive
nothing angelic

Dancing

auras are colors
amber your's, along with pink
pulls me ever deep

my love, your's delights
crimson and turquoise ring through
dance of majesty

as my steps follow
the rays of your pretty steps
your's ahead of mine

we dance back and forth
circling two, ever changing
laughing and twirling

i won't resist you

our colors meld, how could i

this glow has us high

enjoy the moment

our day in the yellow sun

warm embrace given

stay close in this cold

our warmth is the only way

we become as one

Facets

From the old miner's cut, the teardrop

brignolette

Delivered to the cutter for brilliance

conveyed

On to the jeweler's stone, crystals

adorned

One hundred facets, blue garnet tones

Ancient healer, the cabochon smooth

Black opal and its colors, shift in air

The visceral sight of the sapphire

Elegance paired beauty, will not fare

These stones have a weakness

Calling beyond the artisans cue

He can never cut a facet to match

Myriad of light, gem masters rue

I will drink in your facets, lifetime
through

Recalling them all, symbols I never
knew

Your sides show colors, beyond any
gem

Whether sun, or candle light,
refracting true

There is a place inside of you, only I know

Darkness keeps them from finding it

No sight, only shadows, proud and sure

Black nights blind them, groping for a target

The one difference, separating me from them

One thousand facets, needs and dreams

I see them fully, perfect absence of

light

Everything inside you, given entry,

vivid beams

For Winter

True bane
Winter wind sing
Cutting deeper through us
Her bite will be ended gently
Wait sure

The Weight We Carry

My heart holds infinite love for you

I see you in your darkness

And my heart aches

I want to reach out and hold you

But I am told that I must wait

I pace and fret and worry

But this does nothing for your fate

I reassess and think

For time is on my plate

A fire starts within my heart

And I know just what to do

I will hold your suffering

And help carry all of that weight

I fear this weight will only harm

No matter my attempts, too much

You know the look, the sound I make

Silent heart, dead on all counts

My lips stay sealed until full

Your love for me runs too deep

As you long to hold, and held again

If I knew anything of time however

I would tell you it's forever

In that world, my fate is sealed

This world of nightmare weight you
speak

Gives you both time and reprieve

Keep the fire lit for me, I'll come
home

Second Timothy

They branded us with an X; a
generation crossed off the list. We set
out to answer the questions that our
daddy's missed. We were never
Leary, never worried, never feared
this paper, never scary. We rushed in
to feel the magic they missed, never
went to Frisco, never had a summer of
love. It didn't take a movement, never
made a peep against the governing.
We were only boys, brave enough to
test our acuity, to stretch our delicate
realities.

Lights are flickering
So delightfully melting
Damaging nothing

The music stayed the same, save for
the same minstrels branded as such,
like us. They were merely the grungy
echoes of the Grateful, the acidic
blues, the Pink. Never once did we
think to let them keep these sounds
they missed. Squandered a soundtrack
to the planetary and the solitary.
Aural-aware, careful not to drown in
the notes, to crawl inside and lose the
earth. Our quest for Nirvana, Gardens,
Chains and Pearls was quenched with
every hit, every strum.

Lemons or candy
Such a balance to behold
Delve into the trip

It was as if science had captured us,
reading the unholy texts of a
Twentieth Century Timothy.
Disciples of sorts to a propagating
prophet. We soon found that there
was no difference in our ability, no
sectors opened; only a temporary,
rapacious heightening of the senses.
Sights imagined, time replaying,
confusing, beautiful. We watched the
gators red eyes float by in the bay,
bottles melting, trees breathing. A few
met death in a sense, but were easily

convinced otherwise. The most vital buddy system in place, tethered by agility, each with our own ability.

Leather bound erased
Something like a colored curse
Deep into our nights

Out Of Your Reach

Funny near tears, nature's irony smear

Givers with takers, saints and sinners

Stuck together, can't sever, bewitched

Obverse attractions will never switch

Freedom ever awaits, a lover reached

Forces bind him, eight hundred miles

deep

He never knew of her silent grief

Never conceived of a life unleashed

Everything he knew was caustic true

The light he was drawn to the only

cue

Allegory unveiled, eyes open to her

Arms left burning, no known cure

One alone, the other pinned down

The only two willing, could drown

She is out of his reach by far, away

He will try, hope and die for the day

Open

lonely is not me

I find myself in your gaze

touch me without fear

I reach out for you

a longing in my heart's core

seeking your center

spider-cracks in glass

from center out, you can see

obscured vision, me

open your heart wide

nothing to fear, it's just me

love to give, receive

to hear my blue notes
the narrow path, begging please
with closed eyes, come in

embrace profound, breathe
soft landing, veins of gold, breathe
ever in your love

Promises

We swear to stay until the trouble
comes
Ever believing the love can't be
drowned
Always meant in the most heartfelt
ways
So we stick together as if eternally
bound

Then pass the days, the passion it
wears
Frays at the seam, yet holds like a
shackle
When before nothing mattered,
shattered

These fettered words crumble
committal

We call out the issues of
incompatibility
Compare our failures to statistical
deed
See no harm in living with past ghosts
They always end up as such, no need

So love comes easy, shows up at will
The rest is all a telling, a colored
show
Will we show the inky-dim dark
shades
Or will it be the fleeting bright-tint
halo

When all the new sparks begin to
wane
The testing begins with no fires to
rage
Memory feels nothing of the promises
These commitments made, age to age

Waking

Smut black coffee, number three
It won't work, stuck in a dream
Shake me hard 'til I begin to open
The drugs aren't working on me

Bleach white sunlight, pouring in
Doesn't seem to phase me now
Working on high noon, wake me
This time I've slept, running thin

Crumbled road, street runs wait
This slumbering keeps them quiet
No shit smoking pick-ups around
My fear, eternal night at this rate

I need you to read me, say it back

No more walking past this trance

This heart is still skipping beats

Only you can find me, in my lack

A Name

A name is our only symbol

Makes no difference what

Only the sentiment of its ring

I can adorn her name in flora

Draw a rose garden of letters

Color them with tar black ink

Flush them with dirty water

Still, it remains a mere symbol

Prick my fingers on her thorns

Crimson pictures faded brown

Wrap them in canvas, covered

They sting anyway, no healing

Waiting with my brushes, tired

Those others must be artists

Painting self-destructing prints

When those fade, mine will be

Permanence, infinite strokes

I found them in my soul for you

They never belonged to them

Wholesale heartbreak, unseen

Your name is everything to me

The symbol of my every breath

Days will pass unnoticed, mine

Freeze-frame dizzy dancing

You, around my every gift

Hope waning for your return

Into my burning arms, open

The flowers will bloom like

Spring, indifferent to effect

Whether you return or run

They will be scrawled for you

It is my lot and my gift always

Letters never opened if you like

Day Seven

And on the seventh day, nothing
There is no rest, no light nor life

Still waters are stagnant pools
Infectious germ riddled death

This gentle breeze blows toxic
Gamma infused, sick invisible

Strained as Atlas, weight stuck
The only weight hangs in the air

Thousand year scapegoat gone
I see ten million passing around

The earth never rested or slept
Not set into motion with a toss

Not of hand but of empty faith
Creation creative, all its own

So rest all seven, next go 'round
Save us with healings unfound

Let the diseased men prosper not
Curse 'your' leaders to failure true

Step aside and watch us all burn
Never was an alternative for hell

Straight backed, born destructive
Save the work of your dark brutes

We are wired to destruct a habitat
No need for a savior's interruption

Wait for day eight to land down here

There will be no rest for your minions

No church to save all your millions

Only another day to watch it burn

No more story books to ease you

We'll make it fine without the three

Unholy, sick, dead, you'll leave us be

May we return to swamps devolved

There is no more room for your trinity

Entreat Me

The wind blows our words away

We have only been given this day

With the veil torn, eyes can see

Our souls touch, wild and free

It we were to stand far apart

The wind, these words, will stay

Sinking in, linking again, I agree

But souls are trapped, none to see

Far apart? Nay, I say

Come close and feel my embrace

Is it too hot for your skin so fair?

Come on lover, take my dare

Since you insist in this way

My soul lies dormant every day

What man can refuse heat this way?

I challenge you, ready for my pace

Oh, now you want to dance

Come closer, take a chance

Hold me close, keep me safe

How can I lose in your embrace?

Steam like a teapot, bleary eyed

Willing to let my hands stray

Toss safety aside, slide, ride

Closer still, the chance I take

Breathless in your arms, all I feel

Inhale you, intoxicated further still

Your lips touch mine in sweet bliss

My lover, you have answered my

wish

Her Element

If I was able, I would disappear like
you
I would lurk in my element, hidden
true

Impossibility for a single color, mine
For I am hued in many colors, find

Barren, I blend with nature obtuse
If a bird's prey hunted, skin, no use

Sullied by flesh, could live in fear
No form outside, caught clear

You have a keen way of surviving all
With the wings of a leaf, slow crawl

You even possess the power of flight
Delicate, capable legs propel from
fright

No available weapons, cannot defend
She has no need, eclipsed, perfect
blend

Exposed by my figure, naturally
impure
If not for man's reason, my end
assured

Heart Surgery

Your missing voice robs my mind

Black and white nightmare, words

decline

Clouded life behind, would beg for

time

It seems as though I would heal faster

If I were able to erase the passion

A slice, a cut and a fresh wound

I can sew the tears on my own

I'll clean the blood before it dries

Evidence gone, your fault drown

Sad it comes to this, leaving's not

enough

No distance will cure what's in me

Improbable, not fighting, not tough

Surgical precision didn't work

Hearts exhausted, where to now?

Paradise sounded good, overgrown

This cold desert is where we dwell

Silent war, factions, lines drawn

Seems a good time to move on

Child Of The Night

He was stripped of his freedom in the
daylight

Forced to steal it from his keeper in
the night

His eyes grew keen as he walked the
darkness

Found strength in the fear that gripped
him alone

He spent his days slaving in the
gardens of theirs

To eat was his payment, never free to
play in sun

The night became his companion,
then his will

A thief of the master's making he did
become

Hiding

a word can go far
will take your mind off of this
hold you in safety

a book further still
as long as they are written
spilling out of you

a lifetime of words
printed with an aching hand
all gone behind you

we know it's easy
to slip in behind the page
hiding your beauty

Come In

I'll come in when you get there
Doors are open, let yourself in
We must be quiet, no alarm
Tonight we escape to nowhere
Locked in, no chance of harm
The room is safe, heir of implication
Speak to me in your crying whispers
Hearts on the table, two open books
Shredded true, bruised blue hue
Is there really another brand?
If we entered a moment sooner
There would be no surrender
This alliance, long ago rendered
Recalling our secrets comes first
Next comes confession, then a turn
Lying in wait, fires will soon burn
No scents left but our desire merging
This decadent incense of our making

Cast Of The Canvas

Awakened on the hour of three

Most curious musing set free

A lover, my wonder, a craft I see

With canvas mounted, colors arrayed

My approach this night, portrait

stayed

These strokes I commit, brushes

frayed

Shall I paint her in the burning tones

of red

Or soothe her hushed spirit, laurel

green stead

My reception to her chambers surely

depend

Impressionist, abstract, so many to

choose

Will it be quill, dagger or wisp that I

use

This brush particular to palette, her

muse

A lovers desire, longing, hard to bend

One stroke of fault, neglect, never

mend

My brush, the sash, delicacy lend

She is still sleeping, but I hear her call

Fingertip brush strokes, depicting a

doll

This piece should speak of cooling

Fall

Carving Stones

Scraping shapes with tiny knives
Became my way of moving on
The stones are solid indeed
Never mind, time is no need
I plan to grind a sculpture
Intricate, fine, with finesse
No choice not to love it
My life depends on it
Most say, I am out of mind
Can it be you who is mad?
Are your eyes covered blind?
I carve these stones, as one day
The day I am done will be praised
Not with riches or false love
They will perceive my work clear
No question of skill, my dear
To toil with tools, all unfit
No hammer, no chisel

Not a single one of the trade
Commits me not of record
But of a longsuffering heart
I shall carve a swallow
Imagine it's top is blue
I will carve his freedom
Into his whistle and wings
Taking forever, maybe more
My plodding task may lead
To my unfinished craft
My end could come first
If I am to leave before
With my tiny knife in tow
May it be another artisan
Who has the patience I do
One to cause the Swallow
To open her wings and fly

The Teacup

I've a broad platter full of many
choices
My daily bread, or maybe my daily
vice
I may fill it to overflowing with my
fears
I may also serve all of my life's
delights
Most often it is filled with wild
fancies
May my shelter remain in a dry state
Will my children be clothed yet again
No matter what I am served this day
There is sure to be a vacancy for you
For I have not a fear of losing my love
No fruit in season for fear without her
A simple task, scraping away the sour
When morning comes I place her
aside

In a teacup of the most exquisite kind
Sought out with a most delicate hand
And bought not with coin, but my
heart
Surely it's keeper will keep me beside
I've no doubt of the loyalty she brings
So I clear her from my platter of fears

Her

love
colored, fluid
pushing, pulling, changing
like the view of a fast moving
landscape
her

The Hummer's Lady

There's a man I know with music
in his soul
It may be in his brain as well, who
knows
He knows the greats as if he wrote
them all
All alone, his master works spiral
about
Of course no man is capable of
creating
Impossible to have concocted so
many
This man though, loves to pretend
So he hums all the day, no matter
who's around
Some classics, some ethereal, even
folk
In his hope, he will hum into a
woman's heart
His humming grows slowly

emphatic

His own girl to share it with, dual tunes

There must be one who can hum as well

Willing to mumble songs along to a tune

She must be liberated, no inhibition

Together, the humming, exhibition grand

This man is not shy, not afraid to ask

Been denied a hundred times, still at it

His queen is out there, willing, daring

She may take the lead and hum for him

Hummer for so long, a lifetime or so

The poor man deserves a break

All he needs now is a pretty
hummer
A dame unashamed, pretend
singing
A man satisfied for the sake of
song

Biography

Jonathan Ojanpera is a freelance journalist, editor and writer of poetry and fiction. He is also an artist, photographer and musician. His introduction to writing came in the form of poetry in his early teens. His work has been featured on several political, poetic and literary websites and books. His work is continually evolving into long form fiction. He was born in Palm Beach, Florida, spent his childhood in Southwest Colorado and now resides in the Deep South with his wife and four daughters. His creativity is drawn from the multi-cultural experiences he has had, growing up in starkly contrasting regions of the US.

Find more of his work at johnnyojanpera.wordpress.com